BREAKING THE MYTH

The Truth About Black

Fatherhood

by C.A. Truthwell

TABLE OF CONTENTS

ISBN (Paperback): 979-8-9930769-0-4

ISBN (eBook): 979-8-9930769-1-1

This is a work of nonfiction. All research, commentary, and narrative examples reflect the author's interpretation of factual history, policy analysis, and lived experience. Any composite stories or names are used for illustrative purposes and do not depict actual individuals unless explicitly noted.

Breaking the Myth is book one of the Myth Trilogy, books two and three to be announced in the future. A three-part series exploring cultural erasure, systemic advocacy, and emotional restoration for families misnamed by silence.

DEDICATION

To the Black Father

Whose love often goes unseen, unheard, unspoken... but never unfelt.

Who wakes before the sun and rests only when his children are safe, fed, and known.

Who carries the burden of generations and the blessing of legacy in the same calloused hands.

To the one who taught discipline without violence, who gave hugs that healed shame.

Those who stood in courtrooms misjudged and in classrooms overlooked yet still showed up again and again.

This is for the father who raised other men's children as his own.

Who mentored, who mended, who made do.

Those who answered questions with wisdom, pain with patience, silence with presence.

For the ones behind bars who never stopped writing, never stopped calling, never stopped praying.

For the ones working two shifts and still reading bedtime stories over the phone.

For grandfathers, godfathers, big brothers, uncles, stepfathers, and soul-fathers.

Every man who said with his actions, "I will not disappear."

This book is for you.

For the father's history forgot, but children remember.

For the love that exists even when systems say it shouldn't.

For the proof that you were never the problem, only the solution never counted.

I see you. I honor you.

And may this story lift the weight, light the path, and

break the silence forever.

PREFACE

They say stories shape nations more than statistics ever could.

And for far too long, one story has shaped public imagination, policy, and perception.

That Black fathers are absent. Indifferent. A problem to solve.

This book is born from the tension between that story and the lived reality of men I know, men I've stood beside, and the man I am.

Fathers who rise before dawn and walk into systems built to ignore them.

Fathers who whisper affirmations at bedtime and show up to parent-teacher conferences despite being overlooked by courts and coverage alike.

Fathers who carry legacy in their bones, even when society tries to erase them.

What you'll read here isn't theory. It's lived truth. It's bruised but unbowed. Its statistical clarity wrapped in narrative warmth.

I wrote this not to argue, but to reveal. Not to defend, but to honor.

Because once you know the truth, the myth can't survive its silence.

This book is for the fathers who kept loving through distance and doubt.

For the children searching for a fuller story.

And for the communities ready to reclaim the narrative.

Let this preface be the crack in the wall.

The real story starts now.

INTRODUCTION

More Than a Myth

There's a story that's been told about Black fathers in America.

Not a quiet story. Not an evolving one.

It's loud. Repeated. Inherited.

Whispered in courtrooms and classrooms.

Printed in headlines. Played for laughs in sitcoms.

Taught in policy briefings.

And it goes something like this:

"Black fathers are missing."

"They don't care."

"They are the problem."

This story is tidy.

It's convenient.

And it's dangerously incomplete.

Because for every headline about absence, there are thousands of fathers showing up:

At parent-teacher conferences.

On overnight shifts and early-morning daycare drop-offs.

In barbershops, at basketball games, during bedtime routines, and in whispered prayers.

This book began as a contradiction. As a father, I am present, but the world acts like I don't exist.

As a community member, I know men parenting with purpose, but they aren't on TV or in policy agendas.

As a Black man, I feel the tension between the love I live and the narrative I carry.

So, I started digging.

Not just into statistics, but into silence.

Not just into policy, but into pain.

And what I found was louder than any myth.

I found resilience, forged in systems built to break it.

I found tenderness, tucked behind stoic eyes.

I found grandfathers, godfathers, uncles, and cousins,

stepping up, leaning in, refusing to be erased.

This book is not a plea.

It's not a pitch for perfection.

And it's certainly not a defense.

It's an offering. A conversation. A correction.

It's truth, told loud enough to shake loose the lie.

The myth of the absent Black father is powerful.

But so are we.

CHAPTER ONE

The Lie and Its Legacy

"If you repeat a lie often enough, people will start to believe it. But when that lie becomes policy, it stops being just a belief, it becomes a weapon."

America has always had a complicated relationship with the truth, especially when that truth threatens the systems built on inequality. And few lies have traveled further or inflicted more harm than the myth of the absent Black father.

Before we can correct the record, we have to understand how the story got so twisted.

The idea that Black men are chronically irresponsible, detached from their children, inherently less committed to family, isn't just inaccurate, it's manufactured.

And like all successful propaganda, it has roots in policy, politics, and power.

He Was Never Gone.

The day they took him, Mary was five.

She remembers the smell of pancakes, the faded Navy hoodie he always wore, and the way he kissed her forehead twice, once for her, once for good luck.

He didn't come back that night.

Or the next.

Or the one after that.

At school, her teacher asked who lived at home with her.

Mary drew a house with two stick figures: her and her mom. Underneath, she wrote, "My dad lives far away, but not because he wants to."

She never said the word prison out loud. She didn't have to.

Everyone assumed he'd left.

That he didn't care.

That he had never really been there to begin with.

But Mary remembered.

He wrote her letters every week, folded into neat triangles. She saved them in a shoebox. They smelled like ink and hope.

"You were never alone," one said. "They just took me farther than my arms could reach."

Mary was never fatherless. She was just separated from a man she loved, from a story no one ever bothered to tell right.

The Birth of a Dangerous Lie

The absent Black father trope didn't appear out of thin air. It was strategically nurtured.

In 1965, sociologist and Assistant Secretary of Labor Daniel Patrick Moynihan published The Negro Family: The Case for National Action, later known as the Moynihan Report.

The report argued that the disintegration of the Black family, not racism, not poverty, was the central barrier to Black progress. It described Black families as trapped in a "tangle of pathology," placing the blame on absent fathers and dominant mothers.

While Moynihan expressed concern for Black families under economic stress, the report laid the foundation for pathologizing Black fatherhood.

Though Moynihan claimed his goal was to prompt federal support, the language did something else:

It blamed matriarchal households and "emasculated" men for economic hardship.

It fueled a cultural panic that equated single motherhood with national decline.

It portrayed Black men as passive, irresponsible, or emasculated.

It ignored the systemic forces of housing discrimination, joblessness, underfunded schools, and police violence.

This report didn't open a path toward healing.

It opened a trapdoor to blame.

When Being Present Meant Penalty

In the aftermath of the Moynihan Report, welfare rules began to reflect its assumptions.

Federal and state policies included the now-infamous "Man in the House" rule.

Welfare recipients, often single mothers, were subject to surprise inspections, and if a man's belongings were found, their benefits could be revoked.

Fathers were literally pushed out to keep food on the table, not because they didn't want to stay, but because staying meant their children would suffer.

These policies didn't just ignore Black fathers,

they criminalized their presence and punished their love.

How Stereotypes Become Systems

When the myth becomes accepted truth, it begins to shape the world:

In policy: Black fathers face child support enforcement systems that punish poverty with jail time.

In schools: Black boys are labeled "at risk" before they're old enough to write their names.

In media: Black Fatherhood is reduced to punchlines and mugshots, instead of real stories of resilience.

In communities: Black Men feel pressure to perform hypermasculinity, or risk being seen as "soft" or "absent."

A 2022 report from the Urban Institute found that over 60% of Black fathers facing child support arrears earned below the poverty line, yet were more likely to have their licenses suspended or be jailed for nonpayment, compared to white fathers in the same income bracket.

This isn't about morality.

It's about inequality.

It's about how myths become mechanisms.

The Personal Cost of a Public Lie

When you are constantly told you don't exist, or that your existence is a problem, it begins to shape your identity:

Black fathers second-guess their worth.

Children internalize narratives of abandonment.

Communities carry invisible grief.

In researching this book, I learned that Black men felt invisible, not only to society, but sometimes even to their own families, because love without proximity gets labeled as failure.

"I was sending money, calling, writing, but I still got treated like a ghost," said one father. "It's like love only counts if it comes with a key to the front door."

But love isn't limited by ZIP code.

And presence isn't just physical, it's emotional, spiritual, intentional.

Cue the War on Drugs

Launched in the late 1970s and escalated in the 1980s, the War on Drugs wasn't just about narcotics, it was a national strategy that disproportionately targeted Black communities.

Under Presidents Nixon and Reagan, it became a system of mass incarceration built on racial coding and political gain.

Policies like mandatory minimum sentencing, "three strikes" laws, and the 100-to-1 crack-to-powder cocaine disparity meant that a nonviolent drug offense could land someone in prison for decades.

From 1980 to 2000:

The number of Black men incarcerated for drug offenses increased by over 500%.

Black men were 3.6 times more likely to be arrested for drug offenses than white men, despite using at comparable rates.

By the early 2000s, 1 in 9 Black children had a parent behind bars, most often, a father.

Fathers were pulled from their homes not because they abandoned their families, but because their government did.

The Media Played Along

While the courts handled the removal, the cameras took care of the story.

Shows like COPS, sensationalized nightly news clips, and even sitcoms repeated a singular image: the Black father as either a threat or a punchline.

When Barack Obama emerged with a loving, visible family, many mainstream commentators treated it like an anomaly, as if devotion and Blackness rarely occupied the same home.

Statistically, by 1990, Black Americans made up 30% of those arrested for drug offenses yet, accounted for over 60% of those shown in crime-related media.

This was not accidental.

This was narrative control.

The Data Tells a Different Story

In 2013, the Center for Disease Control and prevention (CDC) released a study that shattered the myth:

Black fathers who live with their children were more likely than white and Hispanic fathers to bathe, dress, feed, and play with their children daily.

Among non-custodial fathers, Black dads reported higher levels of day-to-day contact than other racial groups.

In other words, the truth has never matched the myth.

But myths, especially convenient ones, die hard.

Not Just a Correction, a Reckoning

This isn't just about correcting facts.

It's about repairing stories.

Because a false story, when repeated enough, doesn't just misinform. It shapes policy.

It justifies arrests.

It encourages abandonment by assumption.

It tells generations of children that love left, when it never did.

And when a lie this deep gets into law, into airwaves, into the very way a nation sees an entire group of fathers, it becomes a cage.

Breaking the Frame

This book isn't here to argue that every father is perfect.

But it is here to argue that every father is more than a statistic.

And that Black fatherhood, in all its complexity and courage, deserves to be seen.

The myth of absence isn't just wrong, it's violent.

It robs people of their story, their dignity, their lineage.

It turns love into an anomaly.

It turns the truth into an exception.

But here's what we know:

Black fathers are among the most involved in their children's lives across demographic lines.

They navigate structural barriers with quiet brilliance, creating care in spite of chaos.

They deserve policy that reflects their presence, not punishes their poverty.

And they deserve stories that honor their humanity.

That's why truth-telling is powerful.

It doesn't just rewrite the record; it reclaims the future.

CHAPTER TWO

The Numbers Never Lied, We Just Weren't Listening

For decades, the myth of the absent Black father persisted, not because of a lack of data, but because of a lack of will to see it.

The CDC's 2013 National Health Statistics Report revealed something powerful:

70% of Black fathers who lived with their children bathed, diapered, or helped them use the toilet every day.

78% played with their children daily.

63% ate meals with their children every day.

45% read to their children at least several times a week.

These numbers were higher than, or comparable to, those of white and Hispanic fathers.

Yet the dominant narrative remained unchanged.

Why?

Because data doesn't drive culture, stories do.

And the stories we tell about Black men have long been shaped by fear, not fact.

The Census Trap

The U.S. Census Bureau has historically measured fatherhood through household structure.

If a father doesn't live in the same home as his child, he's often not counted as "present" even if he's actively involved.

This method erases:

Divorced or separated fathers with joint custody.

Fathers who live nearby but not in the same household.

Incarcerated fathers who maintain contact.

Fathers in informal co-parenting arrangements.

It's a flawed lens that turns proximity into presence, and absence into assumption.

What Gets Measured Gets Funded

When policymakers rely on flawed data, they create flawed solutions.

Programs designed to support "fatherless" homes often ignore the fathers who are trying to stay involved.

Funding goes to crisis response, not prevention.

And fathers who need job training, legal support, or mental health care are left out of the equation.

We don't need more programs that assume Black men are missing.

We need programs that recognize they're already here, and need support, not suspicion.

The Real Barriers

When Black fathers are struggling, it's not because they don't care.

It's because they're navigating:

Employment discrimination: Studies show that Black men with identical résumés to white applicants are less likely to get callbacks.

Housing instability: Fathers without stable housing often lose custody or visitation rights.

Criminal justice entanglement: Even minor offenses can lead to long-term barriers to employment and parenting.

Family court bias: Many fathers report feeling dismissed or disadvantaged in custody proceedings.

These aren't personal failings.

They're systemic obstacles.

The Cost of Being Counted Out

When fathers are erased from the data, they're erased from the solution.

And when children grow up hearing that their fathers didn't care, when in fact, they were fighting to stay connected, it creates a wound that statistics can't heal.

We need to stop asking, "Where are the fathers?"

And start asking, "What systems are keeping them from being seen?"

CHAPTER THREE

Black Mothers: Holding the Line, Holding the
Truth

You can't talk about Black fatherhood without honoring Black motherhood.

Because while the myth of the absent father has dominated headlines.

Black mothers have been holding the line, raising children, defending their partners, and carrying stories no one asked them to tell.

They've been the translators, the protectors, the bridge between love and loss.

The Myth Hurts Mothers Too

When society assumes that Black fathers are absent, it places an unfair burden on mothers:

They're expected to do it all, without complaint, without help, without rest.

They're blamed for "choosing the wrong man" or "driving him away."

They're denied support because the system assumes they're used to doing it alone.

This isn't empowerment.

Its abandonment dressed up as resilience.

Mothers Who Know the Truth

I've spoken to mothers who've stood in courtrooms defending the father of their child, not because he was perfect, but because he was present.

"I had to lie to the social worker," one mother told me.

"If I said he was helping, they'd cut my benefits. But he was there.

Every night.

Reading to our son.

Cooking dinner.

Just not on paper."

Another mother said,

"They told me I was a single mom. I told them, 'I'm not single, I'm unsupported.' There's a difference."

These women aren't just raising children.

They're raising the truth.

Co-Parenting in the Shadows

Many Black families practice informal co-parenting arrangements that don't fit neatly into legal categories but work in real life.

Fathers who pick up their kids after school every day but don't live in the home.

Mothers who rely on their child's father for emotional support, discipline, and guidance.

Grandparents, aunts, uncles, and godparents who form a network of care.

These networks are strong, but they're invisible to systems that only recognize nuclear families.

The Emotional Toll

When fathers are erased, mothers are left to carry the emotional labor of explaining an absence that isn't real.

They have to answer questions like:

"Why doesn't Daddy live here?"

"Does he still love me?"

"Did I do something wrong?"

And when the answer is, "He's trying, but the system won't let him," there's no checkbox for that on a school form.

Mothers as Witnesses

Black mothers have been the quiet witnesses to this erasure.

They've seen the love.

They've seen the struggle.

They've seen the system work against the very men they're told to distrust.

And still, they hold space.

They hold memories.

They hold the line.

This chapter is for them.

Because breaking the myth of the absent Black father also means breaking the silence around the mothers who've been telling the truth all along.

CHAPTER FOUR

Systems of Separation: How Policy Keeps Fathers Away

It's not enough to say Black fathers are present.

We have to ask: what's keeping them from being seen, supported, and sustained?

The answer isn't just cultural.

It's structural.

Family Court Isn't Built for Fathers

Many Black fathers describe the family court system as a maze designed to wear them down:

Filing for custody or visitation often requires legal knowledge and fees that many can't afford.

Courts tend to favor mothers in custody decisions, especially when fathers aren't married to the child's mother.

Fathers who fall behind on child support, often due to unemployment or underemployment, can face jail time, license suspension, or wage garnishment.

One father told me, "I missed one court date because I couldn't get off work. They issued a warrant. I wasn't a criminal, I was a dad trying to keep my job."

Child Support as Punishment

The child support system was created to ensure children receive financial support, but in practice, it often punishes poverty.

Noncustodial Black fathers are more likely to be unemployed or underemployed.

Many are assigned support orders based on imputed income, not actual earnings.

Falling behind can lead to jail, which only makes it harder to pay.

This creates a cycle: poverty → arrears → incarceration → deeper poverty.

It's not about "deadbeat dads." It's about a system that treats financial struggle as moral failure.

Incarceration as Family Policy

The U.S. has the highest incarceration rate in the world, and Black men are disproportionately affected.

1 in 3 Black boys born today can expect to be incarcerated in his lifetime if current trends continue

Over 2.7 million children in the U.S. have a parent in prison or jail.

Black children are 7.5 times more likely than white children to have an incarcerated parent.

This isn't just a criminal justice issue. It's a family issue. A fatherhood issue.

And when incarceration is treated as a solution to poverty, addiction, or trauma, it becomes a policy of separation.

Housing and Employment Discrimination

Even after release, formerly incarcerated fathers face:

Housing bans from public housing authorities.

Employment discrimination due to criminal records.

Loss of voting rights, limiting their ability to advocate for change.

These barriers don't just impact individuals, they affect entire families.

The Cost of Being Present

For many Black fathers, being present means navigating a system that punishes them for trying.

Showing up in court without a lawyer.

Taking jobs that pay under the table to avoid wage garnishment.

Living apart from their children to prevent benefit cuts for the mother.

Fighting for visitation while being labeled "uninvolved"

Presence shouldn't be a penalty. But for too many, it is.

We Need Policy That Reflects Reality

If we want to support Black fatherhood, we need to:

Reform child support to reflect actual income and prioritize co-parenting.

End incarceration for nonpayment of support.

Provide legal aid for fathers navigating custody and visitation.

Ban housing and employment discrimination based on criminal history.

Fund fatherhood programs that center dignity, not deficiency.

Because the problem isn't that Black fathers are absent, it's that the system is designed to make them disappear.

CHAPTER FIVE

What the Data Really Says

Let's break down the numbers that rarely make headlines:

CDC Fatherhood Involvement Study (2013)

Among fathers who live with their children (Age 5-18):

Among non-residential fathers, Black dads were more likely than white or Hispanic dads to:

Talk to their children on a daily basis

Help with homework.

Attend school events.

Pew Research Center (2011)

Black fathers were more likely than white or Hispanic fathers to report involvement in key caregiving tasks.

They were also more likely to say they bathed, dressed, or helped their children use the toilet daily.

Urban Institute (2022)

Over 60% of Black fathers with child support arrears earned below the poverty line.

Black fathers were more likely to face punitive enforcement actions than white fathers in similar financial situations.

National Responsible Fatherhood Clearinghouse (2023)

Black fathers are more likely to participate in fatherhood programs than any other racial group.

These programs report high levels of engagement, retention, and success among Black men.

What It All Means

The data is clear:

Black fathers are deeply involved in their children's lives.

They face systemic barriers that distort their presence.

They are not the exceptions; they are the evidence.

We don't need more studies. We need more truth-telling. More policy rooted in reality. More stories that reflect the love.

CHAPTER SIX

The Role of Media: Who Tells the Story?

If policy is the skeleton of the myth, media is its skin. It gives the lie a face, a voice, and a soundtrack.

The Absent Father Trope

From sitcoms to news broadcasts, the image of the Black father has often been reduced to:

The deadbeat dad.

The criminal.

The emotionally distant patriarch.

The comedic buffoon.

Rarely do we see the full, complex, loving, flawed, and present Black father.

News Media and Crime Coverage

Studies show that Black suspects are disproportionately featured in crime coverage, while white suspects are more likely to be shown in humanizing ways, through family photos, community involvement, or personal backstories.

This imbalance shapes both public perception and policy.

When we see Black men on the news in handcuffs, the image becomes easier to believe they're absent from their children's lives.

Entertainment Media

Even in fictional portrayals, Black fatherhood is often sidelined:

In dramas, the father is missing or abusive.

In comedies, he's reduced to a punchline.

In reality TV, he's barely present.

There are exceptions, Black-ish, This Is Us, and Queen Sugar, but they remain just that: exceptions.

The Power of Representation

Representation isn't just about visibility. It's about possibility.

When children see loving, engaged Black fathers on screen, it broadens their sense of what's normal, and what's possible.

When fathers see themselves reflected with dignity, it affirms both their efforts and their humanity.

We Need New Storytellers

To change the narrative, we need:

More Black writers, producers, and directors.

More documentaries and books that center real fatherhood.

More platforms that amplify community voices.

Because the myth didn't start with facts, it started with stories. And it will end with better ones.

CHAPTER SEVEN

Healing the Wound: What Families Need

Breaking the myth isn't just about correcting the record, it's about healing the harm.

Because when a lie this big goes unchecked, it leaves scars:

Children who grow up believing they were abandoned

Fathers who internalize shame and silence.

Mothers who carry the weight of two roles without recognition.

What Children Need

Children don't need perfect fathers.

They need present ones.

Consistency

Emotional availability.

Protection and guidance.

Affirmation of their worth.

And they need systems that support, not sabotage, those relationships.

What Fathers Need

Access to their children.

Legal support for custody and visitation.

Mental health resources to process trauma.

Job training and employment opportunities.

Community spaces where they're seen and supported.

What Mothers Need

Systems that don't force them to choose between support and honesty.

Recognition of co-parenting dynamics.

Relief from the pressure to do it all alone.

Healing from the emotional labor of navigating broken systems.

What Communities Need:

Fatherhood initiatives that are culturally competent and trauma informed.

Schools that engage fathers, not just mothers.

Churches, barbershops, and community centers that affirm fatherhood.

Media that reflects the truth, not the trope.

Healing Is Possible

I've seen it.

I've seen fathers reunite with children after years of separation.

I've seen mothers and fathers co-parent with grace and grit.

I've seen young men become the fathers they never had.

I've seen communities rally around men who were once written off.

Healing is not hypothetical. It's happening. But it needs support.

Because love alone isn't always enough. It needs policy. It needs protection. It needs truth.

CONCLUSION

The Truth Was Always There

The myth of the absent Black father is one of the most persistent lies in American culture. But it's not just a lie, it's a weapon. One used to justify broken policies, fractured families, and generational pain.

But here's the truth:

Black fathers are present.

Black fathers are loving.

Black fathers are essential.

They always have been.

This book is not the end of the conversation. It's the beginning of a reckoning.

Because when we tell the truth loudly, clearly, unapologetically, we don't just correct the record. We reclaim the future.

EPILOGUE

To My Brothers

To every Black man who has ever been told he's not enough, this is for you.

To the fathers who stayed, even when no one saw you.

To the fathers who left and came back.

To the fathers who are trying, learning, healing.

To the men who father through mentorship, through presence, through love.

You are not invisible.

You are not a statistic.

You are not a myth.

You are the proof.

You are the legacy.

You are the truth.

And the world needs your story.

ACKNOWLEDGMENTS

To my family, thank you for being the foundation, the fire, and the faith behind every word.

To fathers who continually share their stories with others, your vulnerability is a gift. Your truth is sacred.

To the mothers who held the line, your strength is unmatched, your love undeniable.

To every child who ever wondered why their father wasn't there, may this book help you see that love often lives in silence, in struggle, and in systems that tried to keep it out.

To communities all over, thank you for believing in this work, for challenging the system, and for reminding policy makers that truth-telling is a form of resistance. And to the reader, thank you for choosing to see beyond the myth.

May this book be a mirror, a map, and a movement.

RESOURCES & NOTES

Organizations Supporting Black Fathers and Families

National Fatherhood Initiative -

https://www.fatherhood.org

Center for Urban Families - https://www.cfuf.org

Fathers Incorporated -

https://www.fathersincorporated.com

The Black Father Foundation -

https://www.blackfatherfoundation.org

National Responsible Fatherhood Clearinghouse -

https://www.fatherhood.gov

The Bail Project - https://www.bailproject.org

Equal Justice Initiative - https://www.eji.org

The Sentencing Project -

https://www.sentencingproject.org

Urban Institute - https://www.urban.org

Pew Research Center - https://www.pewresearch.org

CDC National Center for Health Statistics -

https://www.cdc.gov/nchs

INDEX

ABOUT THE AUTHOR

C.A. Truthwell is the pen name of Clayton A. Francis, a retired U.S. Navy veteran and devoted father whose disciplined mind and compassionate heart fuel his mission to challenge the stereotypes that have long distorted the image of Black fatherhood. Writing under a name that reflects both clarity and conviction, Truthwell blends lived experience, rigorous research, and a deep commitment to justice.

He is the author of Breaking the Myth, book one of the Myth Trilogy, books two and three to be announced in the future. A three-part series exploring cultural erasure, systemic advocacy, and emotional restoration for families misnamed by silence.

Truthwell's work is part of a broader movement to reclaim truth, restore dignity, and inspire generational change.

Connect with the Author

Your journey through Breaking the Myth is only the beginning.

To stay informed about upcoming books, exclusive content, community conversations, and the movement behind the message, connect with C.A. Truthwell online:

Website:

www.catruthwell.com

Instagram:

@author_catruthwell

Facebook:

facebook.com/catruthwell

Purchase More Works:

catruthwell.gumroad.com

Professional Inquiries

Email: author@catruthwell.com

Whether you're a reader, a father, an advocate, or a believer in change, thank you for being part of this journey.

The truth is here, and you're a part of it.